D1744110

GOD WHERE IS MY BOAZ?

HOW TO FIND YOUR SOUL MATE:
HOW TO FIND MR RIGHT: MATURE CHRISTIAN WOMEN

By Nicola Gayle

ISBN: 9781519067715

A wife of noble character is her husband's crown, but a
disgraceful wife is like decay in his bones.

Proverbs 12:4

You Can Contact Me At

nicolagayle63@gmail.com

Contents

$\mathcal{I}$ was 21, excited about life and new relationships. I grew up in the church and was taught how to choose a mate and the Godly rules I should follow to live a great Christian life. These rules I tried my utmost to follow so that I could get my Boaz and enjoy my marriage while living a Christ-filled life.

But all those rules that I followed never helped to buffer me from a broken heart and a life filled with disappointments. As I looked around and started observing some of my Christian friends, I realized we were all in the same boat.

A cycle of cheap romances that never lasted, we were all damaged emotionally and very insecure. What made it even worst I was trying to remain celibate protecting my virginity which never encouraged my "Christian" boyfriends to stay.

My desperation for change motivated me to pray. I have been a Christian for as long as I can remember, as I got older the realization hit me that God was never front and center in my life. I have always said that God was my highest priority, but truthfully, I was more distracted and focused on guys and my social status.

I never saw anything wrong with how I choose to live my life.

What was wrong with my life?

What was wrong with how I was living?

I was going to church, I was dating Christian guys at least that's what they called themselves. I was also committed to not having sex before marriage.

When I think about it my life was more moral than most of my other "Christian friends." Even though God wasn't front and center in my daily life, I thought I was on good terms with God.

But my heart was broken over and over again and I had to take a step back and ask myself what was I doing wrong.

After being in a relationship that looked promising the guy broke it off, I was devastated depression and confusion set in, I remember crying out to God for answers.

"God, what am I doing wrong?" I moaned, the hurt was real.

"I've been a good Christian I have followed all the dating principles. Why do all my relationships end up this way?"

While asking the questions and feeling the hurt I felt a moment of peace. I suddenly knew that my life didn't have to be this way, God had something better for me. All I had to do was trust Him.

Whenever we try to do things our way it will never work, going out and trying to find your Boaz without the blessings of God will cause you to be hurt many times over. Never try to write your love story alone trust God to do it for you. Allow God to be the center of your existence.

But how do I give God total and complete control of my life, especially my love life? I don't mind obeying certain Christian principles and rules when it comes to dating, as long as I am in control of choosing my Boaz.

But trusting God and letting go of my right to make my own decisions about who I dated was something else.

Was I ready to give God control? God wanted me to trust Him, not kind of trust Him, not conditionally trust Him but just let go and allow Him to write my love story.

What if I allowed God to send my Boaz and He never sends me anyone? Or direct me to someone I wasn't attracted to?

I remember being in church and heard the Pastor saying he got a vision that a certain young lady was supposed to get married to a young paralyzed guy. She was very responsive to the vision the pastor had, so they got married but for me, if that was a prophecy for my life it would have been after some deep consultation with God and not just second-hand directions from my local pastor.

My fears grew more every day and my questions increased. We all say we trust God, but do we? Are you someone who says "God if it is Your will let it be done" and mean it? Because whenever I say that, deep down I still pray and hope that Gods will is aligned with mine. The one thing I knew without the shadow of a doubt was that I wasn't doing a good job in that department if I continued I would only have more heartache, broken promises and attending weddings of ex-boyfriends. Truth be told it was more out of desperation than confidence in God that I "trusted God"

with my love life.

Ruth & Boaz

*T*he story of Ruth and Boaz has been told for many generations and has inspired many women. I have sat down for many years alone reading my Bible studying the word you may know the story already but if not let's take a walk down memory lane.

*   *   *

It was the time of harvest in Israel when Boaz first saw this beautiful young woman. The sun shone across the fields leaving a golden glare as the workers swung their sickles in a rhythmic motion through the standing wheat.

The laws and custom of Israel gave the poor rights to gather whatever the harvesters missed. Ruth went through the field quickly gathering and stuffing grains into a sack slung over her shoulder.

Boaz noticed her with strands of black hair creeping under her head covering, she had soft olive colored skin, it was still smooth despite the harsh unrelenting sun.

She rested for only a few minutes, she looked around wary of any sign of trouble from the men harvesting the fields.

Gleaning was hard work, there was also the possibility of lurking danger in the form of harassment. This was even more apparent for a young beautiful foreigner who everyone knew was alone and without protection.

The town of Bethlehem had made the conversation of Boaz's relative Naomi the trending topic because of her unexpected return. Ruth, the beautiful young lady from the field who accompanied her was her daughter-in-law he had learned.

He had heard the story of their tragedy and the unrivaled loyalty the young Ruth had for her mother in law, she had even promised to renounce Moab's idols for Israel's God.

Everyone on earth would wish for a friend as Ruth has been to Naomi. Boaz was determined to reward her for her kindness in any small way he could.

"My daughter, listen to me don't go and glean in another field and don't go away from here. Stay here with my servant girls. Watch the field where the men are harvesting, and follow along with the girls. I have told the men not to touch you." Said Boaz, as he looked at Ruth mesmerized by her beauty.

Ruth smiled and nodded in agreement to the kind gesture. Later that day he spoke to her yet again, this time he showed her more kindness by offering her bread and grains that he had roasted for her dinner.

The kindness shown by Boaz was one that was directly from his heart he had fallen in love with this young beautiful lady but was wary of showing how he felt because he was also much older than her.

When she finished eating, Boaz told his workers to pull some stalks of wheat and scatter them across her path. He felt good watching her leave that evening with her sack bulging; filled with a bountiful harvest.

This continued for many days after. He watched her daily knowing that the wheat and barley harvest would soon come to an end……. he dreaded that day.

Then one fateful evening Boaz and his workers were winnowing barley on the threshing floor. After he had finished, he had dinner, he then laid down at the far end of the pile of grains.

The men also stayed with him because they had to guard the harvest. With all this security, no robber would think of entering and trying to steal.

But in the middle of the night he awoke to a startling discovery he was surprised to find an intruder but the intruder wasn't a robber……wasn't even a man, the intruder was a woman who lay at his feet. She was also awake.

"I am your servant, Ruth" she whispered her voice subtle and delicate.

"Spread the corner of your garment over me, since you are a kinsman-redeemer"

Her words were soft but quite direct Boaz could hardly believe what he was hearing. This young woman was taking a great risk, coming out at night and also lying so close to him.

The request wasn't uttered again as he quickly covered her, saying in a hushed tone, "The Lord bless you. This kindness is greater than that which you showed Naomi: You have not run after the younger men, whether rich or poor."

"And now, my daughter don't be afraid I will do for you all you ask." Ruth lay at his feet rising before daybreak could make her presence known to the others who were there.

Ruth so far has shown bravery that women today rarely shows she knew what she wanted and she went for it. Likewise, when you see your Boaz don't be afraid to go after him there have been many fears of rejection that have left a lot of single Christian women with unwritten or half-written love stories.

Let's get back to the story…..

There are no love stories that are without pitfalls and or obstacles and Boaz and Ruth was no exception. Naomi had a relative who was much closer than Boaz, this man could also assume the role as kinsman-redeemer, getting married to Ruth hence restoring her deceased husband's name.

Boaz cringed and shuddered at the thought of such a scenario. This man was entitled to purchase a field that Naomi owned.

If he purchased that field, by the law of Israel he also was obligated to marry Ruth. Such an outcome would destroy any hope of Boaz having Ruth as his wife.

Boaz could not sleep or wait for such a feared possibility to become a reality so he approached the man and told him about the land he was very interested in acquiring.

But when he heard that he also had to marry Ruth as part of the deal he immediately gave up his rights to purchase the land to Boaz.

Take note Ruth was desired by Boaz from the first day he saw her while the other man wasn't interested in her in the least.

No matter what you may think your Boaz is out there he can see no other woman but you and he desire no other woman but you.

They both got married and the older man welcomed his young beaming bride into his home. The union was blessed by God they had a son named Obed.

We can now imagine how happy they all were. Boaz watched with admiration one day with Ruth by his side as Naomi held her grandson to her breast.
On this particular day, she was surrounded by some of the women of Bethlehem, she was a picture of happiness and pride she glowed with youthful effervescence. She looked so young again this is the woman he remembered when her husband Elimelech was alive.

He watched as the women who surrounded her spoke to her regarding Obed.

"Praise be to the Lord, who this day has not left you without a kinsman-redeemer. May he become famous throughout Israel! He will renew your life and sustain you in your old age for your daughter-in-law, who loves you and who is better to you than seven sons, has given him birth."

Boaz knew that this was the truth Ruth was more valuable to Naomi than seven sons. He felt it in his heart that their friendship was even more beneficial to him.

If Ruth and Naomi had not developed that bond they wouldn't have traveled together and without her, in his life, the happiness he now feels would not have been present.

Boaz felt young again but God had a greater plan than just writing this magnificent love story. Their son Obed, went on to become the father of Jesse, Jesse was the father of King David.

Ruth and Boaz were not only the great-grandparents of King David but they were also mentioned in the family tree of Jesus of Nazareth our own kinsman-redeemer.

Don't lose hope your Boaz is out there.

Are there any Christian single women out there?

I'm Nikki

I guess you are sitting and talking to me today because we have a few things in common, let me fill you in on a little background about my journey.

I had fallen in love, it felt so good even noise sounded like music it was surreal, but that was 25 years ago now I am fifty-two and single, I have "stumbled" into single life.

How did I get here?......... If I knew the answer to that question, then maybe just maybe, I would still be married.

My last child has flown the roost a dreaded reality I had to face because I told her she was ready but in reality, I wasn't; now my house is empty and also my life.

My husband, I still refer to him as because I still haven't gotten used to the idea that I am no longer married; left me for a younger girl, one of the things I hate most about her, she is very pretty, I painfully have to admit.

I was twenty-one yesterday young and in demand, I had more suitors than a princess, I went to bed and got up to no suitors and almost sixty years old.

My husband has left me when no one else saw me as being desirable or think I should dare to still have feelings. People always think that as soon as a woman is over forty and she isn't married she should just go to church and forget about men…….. I easily uttered such sentiments, when I was younger.

I looked around the house everything was in order nothing to clean, no one to shout at or talk to ……no one.

Sunday has come and I have taken out my dress I find myself thinking about my life or whatever you could call it.

"Is this how I will be living for the rest of my life?" I got scared when I heard myself say it out loud.   I was lonely, I got dressed and I was off to church.

I am looking around my Church and almost 60% of the members are single females over forty years old. They say that a man is no longer on their mind but: so is walking when you no longer have legs.

"I really want to get married." These words aren't uttered loudly in many church circles.   They are hushed and spoken only between close friends.   The situation that single Christian women face from both peers and from within is dire.

Christian women today are ashamed to admit that they want to get married. The steps that they need to take are explored later in our conversation, but what you must bear in mind is that it's a combination of things.

For a lot of people, the reason they don't talk about it is that of embarrassment, it hasn't happened yet or they are no longer married.

Of course, me being in the latter category, I often times wondered if something was wrong with me. I no longer have a man asking me out for a date I see other people married but I'm not, I have friends getting married so why not me?

Some of my friends and church sisters have a different mindset they think you're not supposed to want to get married if you are over forty.

As if it's one of those many goals you can get if you want. They tend to talk more about the things they have control over in their life like their job, homes and other material things they can acquire.

The sad truth is marriage is one of the few things that takes two people to get it done, you can't get married alone.

I know a lot of single Christian women.
Where are all the single Christian men?

There is this talk that women outnumber men, but according to research, there are more Christian single men who would love to get married than Christian single women. Now for the big obstacle, try finding them.

The church should try and play a role in sending out the message of how important and sacred marriage is. Hold the single men accountable and not have them dating every single woman in the church, but to make them commit. There needs to be a mentoring of single men in the church by older married men to let them know that they should be looking for a wife and to help them to be the kind of man that would make a good husband.

"I am 45 years old and I have never been married. I have the same perspective and suffered the embarrassment of being ashamed to admit that I would like to be married".

Sheryl looked as if a burden was lifted off her shoulders.

"Now I will be totally honest and say, I would love to be married!" She said it with purpose, and we all knew she meant it.

It was a surprise when Sheryl got up and said it, we were at our weekly prayer meeting that we women who ***don't have a husband to take care of go to***, she looked relieved that she said it.

I am 52 and have wrestled with this for a long time. As a woman, sometimes I feel a double standard in that we cannot even remotely pursue without being labeled in a certain way.

As Christians, I truly hope we can pray for each other as " there is power in united prayer" because there is strength in doing so. We get bogged down in societal pressures, thinking we're flawed, and wondering if God has forsaken us but He hasn't, we have value because God made us.

One thing hopefully we late bloomers have is endurance, gratitude, and compassion. Which in turn will allow us to be good partners who understand just how sacred love is when it's given.

In my experience, single Christians kind of stay on the outer margins but we really should empower each other and support each other.

Just know you're not alone and that we have to be courageous and speak our hearts (*putting it out there as "yes, I too hope to find a life partner, best friend, and husband"*) - Hopefully by Grace, God will allow that person to come into our lives. Meanwhile, we pray fervently for another chance.

The Wedding

My friend Jackie tied the knot recently.

Walking down the aisle, grinning wildly, she winked as she passed me. She was now walking into a new dimension her new season was here she now had her Boaz, a new house, different responsibilities … and sex. The thought of the "S" word made me smile to myself

.

Jackie has never even kissed Frank before they got married. They both wanted to wait until their wedding day or at least that's what Jackie said.

Because of that, their dating had little intimacy, it was just shaking hands a little longer than normal, hugs that never stayed long enough to be called an embrace and they made sure they spent as little time as possible alone.

"All Frank and I do is hold hands and talk", Jackie told me one day over coffee at Starbucks.

(yeah, right and the ocean is really blue! I thought to myself)

Until this day, I shudder at the thought of something like that really being true.

Jackie and I; we were always different women in opinions and what we talk about. I sometimes reminisce on how Jackie and I would talk about sex, life, marriage, men, romance, and sex.

I was always very vocal Jackie would not speak much about sex because everything for her seemed to always go back to her saying it was a sin.

I will never forget the day when I saw a group of "older" Christian women talking and I stopped to ask them about sex. Jackie immediately screamed that she was not interested in that topic she covered her ears and ran off before the ladies happily answered (*sex not being a topic uttered around them anymore ... they had a lot to say*).

I was never the one to be ashamed. I had faith that one day God would send me my Boaz, I wanted to be ready I needed as much information and opinions as possible.

Jackie says that I think about sex too much and I should try and control my sexual urges......that's like telling me to control my breathing, I would prefer a man come and control my sexual urges.
As usual, she thinks my urges are not of God, I think that I am more in tune with God, because what I am feeling is pure feelings created in me by God.

She said I should wait on God for my Boaz......I have been doing that for a while now, so I don't think anything is wrong if I try and meet God along the way.

 Sometimes I truly believe Gods clock is broken where my relationship is concerned. Jackie said I shouldn't talk like that because it doesn't sound Christ-like.

I have been to many Christian gatherings and one that stands out in my mind was where the speaker was a Christian lady, she told us that we should give every single part of our being to God even our sexuality she looked directly into my eyes and said yes especially our sexuality.

The women in the gathering a vast majority being married all nodded in agreement with her pronouncement. I looked around .... That is so easy to say when you have your husband at home. What about the others who were in my situation is celibacy that easy???
I have accepted Jesus Christ as my Lord and Savior for a number of years.
I have no doubt that I love God.
But at times my hormones drives me crazy, desperation sometimes creeps in, I really needed a man to share my life and body with that special God loving man.

I remember sitting there in the gathering wondering and daydreaming about that special person for me, in my carnal mind, among the high-flying group of "flawless Christian ladies".

Many Christians grow up with the mindset that they will just flick that sexual switch when they get married, they all think that their sexuality will remain dormant and asleep only to be awakened by marriage……if only it was that simple

A brute in Boaz clothing…...

$\mathcal{P}$aula had a serious problem which she couldn't see an end to. One night while sitting at home enjoying a cup of coffee I heard a knock on my door.

It was Paula she was a shadow of the woman she used to be. She was unkempt she had a look of quiet desperation, her face was tear stained and swollen. After I ushered her in I offered her coffee which she eagerly accepted.

Her marriage to Robert was one that seemed like it was made in heaven, but this isn't always the case. With trembling hands and crackling tear soaked sentences, she began to tell me about her marriage to Robert who was a prominent member of our church.

"As you know I have been married for over a year now, I saw Robert as the love of my life" her hands were wrapped around the cup she was staring in the coffee as if she was looking for something.

"I was happy, he was loving and caring, he was very kind to me."

"Why do you say was, are you saying he no longer is any of that?"

Three months into our marriage it was my birthday we went out and after returning home we made love. After which I got up and wrote a long and detailed love letter to him on my phone my intention was to text it to him as a loving gesture.

He was on the night shift so he would be leaving soon.

What happened next was nothing short of a nightmare.

He walked over to me after coming out of the shower with just a towel wrapped around his waist and asked,

"What are you doing with your phone?" to that question I answered and told him what I was doing.

"Do you think I am an idiot?" the look in his eyes were of rage.

"You are texting another man and we just had sex?" his fists were clenched, I had never seen this side of him before.

He started hitting me, punching me without mercy I begged him to stop, I pleaded that it was my birthday but he didn't stop.

I cried for the entire night no man had ever hit me before not even my father. I moved out of the matrimonial home still keeping up appearances I went to church and pretended that everything was ok he also wanted to protect his reputation because of the position he holds in church.

For weeks, I couldn't eat or sleep, all I could remember was the senseless beating. He called me every day and begged for forgiveness he said he didn't know that I was texting him and he was sorry.

You must notice in situations like these if he is truly your Boaz he wouldn't and couldn't hurt you no matter what.

This man wasn't sorry about hurting Paula he wasn't apologetic about beating her he said he didn't know that she was texting him.

I decided to try and work on the marriage I don't know if it was because I didn't want to look like a failure or I would be ridiculed by everyone for having such a short marriage, I don't know what it was all I know I decided to take it slow.

He tried his best to make it up to me and I forgave him.

Five months later I was back in the matrimonial home, and that's when all hell broke loose.

Everything I did, this person, this thing whatever it was would beat me for it. I was beaten like a drum.

Through all of this I got pregnant; one night I was coming home from work, a male coworker took me home because it was raining and he saw him drop me off.

As soon as I stepped through the door he started raining blows all over my body, saying I was having an affair with my coworker and he knows the baby isn't his.

That same night I lost the baby from the beating. He cried and said he was sorry.

I decided to start taking contraception and has luck should have it he found the pills in my drawer. He got really upset and started hitting me he grabbed me by my hair and pulled me all over the house. He said he wanted me to have his eight children (*this I didn't even know*) and if he found out that I was still on any pills he would kill me.

All of this was happening to me while I mourned and ached in silence going to church and watching him play the righteous man of God smiling and parading.

I got pregnant again and against the laws of God, I had an abortion. He found out and gave me a beating until I passed out.

I know you must be asking the question why didn't Paula run again?

But she had given up her apartment and fear had also paralyzed her.

As Christian women, often times all we have is each other.   We must find older ladies in the church that we can confide in, speaking to them and getting advice or help can save our lives.

I had to lie to him so that he would stop. I told him that he said he didn't want to have kids right now that's why I did it.

I then decided that I was going to leave him for good I was going to expose him for the dirty man he is I didn't care about how he would look to everyone in the church……..but I got pregnant again.

Five months into the pregnancy we got into another fight I was sick of him beating me so I broke his phone, tablet and his prized guitar.

He got so angry that he threw me to the floor and used a piece of board to beat me across my back, face, belly, and legs. That day I lost my babies……I was expecting twins.

His mother came to visit me at the hospital. Her advice was to leave him because he was an undiagnosed madman a psychopath that she herself was afraid of, she said she knows that he is beating me.

I told her that I would love to leave but he is always home. We both devised a plan in which she would ask him to take her somewhere and I would pack my things and leave.

Three weeks later she told me the date and also hired a U-Haul for me. When he left that day with my heart pounding in my chest I packed all my belongings and moved as fast as I could.

But I was not at peace he came to my place of employment daily always smiling with everyone in his well-tailored suits, giving the impression of a Godly gentleman.

One evening he waited outside for me and held me up with a knife he ordered me in his car, I was viciously raped by him that evening.

He told me to come back home, I told him I would but all I wanted to do was get out of his car alive. He dropped me at the subway station that day and I cried like a grieving mother at a funeral. I didn't care who saw me I was just frustrated.

I left my job and changed my number.
It has been three months since I last saw him. But last night while coming home from my new job as I reached home (to my new place) he just stepped out from almost nowhere and punched me in my face, I was knocked unconscious.

I awoke in his car, my eyes were swollen almost closed, my mouth was bleeding he was crying and accusing me of causing him to hurt me and that I brought out the worst in him.

He said he was going to lock me up in his house and that I had to have his eight kids I couldn't leave because I am his.

He stopped at a church Brothers house to make plans for next Sundays service he had parked the car in the dark because he didn't want anyone to see my bloodied face.

He told me if I left the car he would find me and kill me.

As soon as he left I ran from the car, he caught me and started beating me again, while crying out for help a man came out and told him to leave me alone. That's when I ran straight to your house.

"Knock, knock" someone was at my door.

"Who is it?" I didn't expect anyone.

"It's Robert, may I have a word with you?" he was sounding as calm as ever.

Paula was petrified.

Colossians 3:18-19

18 Wives, submit yourselves to your husbands, as is fitting in the Lord.

The problem with a lot of men is they will read verse 18 and then leave it at that.

But going just one verse down in 19 it completes it.

19 Husbands, love your wives and do not be harsh with them.

What you should look for in your Boaz

He should be a Christian man

*W*hen I say Christian, it shouldn't be just a man who says he believes in God. When I say a Christian man, I am talking about a man that is saved by grace and he is proud of it. This type of man is a proud believer and follower of Christ, he constantly strives to be a Godly man.

He is always working on his relationship with God before he works on any other relationship. This type of Christian man chooses to walk in Gods will for his life and not his own.

He should be a praying man.

A man who knows how to talk to God and always does it. This type of man will always be praying to God in good times and also in times of trials.

Whatever the situation he will know where to turn to get the solutions to his troubling questions and where to give his praise when there are things to give thanks for.

Whenever you find a man that prays he will always be praying for you, your family and also the relationship.

There will also be the need to pray for Gods strength to overcome any weaknesses, temptations or frustrations that he may have.

He should cherish and adore you

*H*e should cherish you no matter what. A man who adores you will protect you, your reputation, your name, and your family.

When you meet a man like this he will let you know you are special and that you are unique and made just for him. You will be treated like the Queen you are.

He should be honest

*H*e shouldn't just be an honest man in his public life, but also a man who is honest with you and honest with himself.

He should know his faults, acknowledges them and is always working on making himself better.

He should be a man of his word whatever he tells you he is going to do he does it. When you meet an honest man, he will never lead you on.

And he will never cause you to become a dishonest woman.

He should have a purpose.

*W*hy would you have a man who isn't driven?

He should be someone who is passionate about something. He should be working towards something uplifting even though this doesn't necessarily equate to success it adds up to the excitement and futurist opportunities.

You come second only to God

*O*nly God should come before you.

Your feelings

Your needs

Your Wants

It doesn't matter, nothing or nobody's feelings should come before yours, not even his. You should never compromise on this, there are no exceptions.

A man who loves you

*H*is love for you should be unconditional. You should never be left in a position to guess how he feels about you.

He shouldn't have to tell you every day because his actions should do all the talking. When you find a man, who loves you he will honor you, respect you and will always stand beside you.

He will always encourage you and will never tear you down. A Godly man will support and encourage you on your path to developing a better relationship with The Almighty God.

How do you know he is right for you?

Is he a good provider?

Even though you are an established mature woman you still want to make sure the man you meet is responsible. Someone you can count on, if at this age, he hasn't found his way in that area then I don't think he has any plans to.

Does he have the willpower to keep a job?

*I*f he hasn't retired as yet, then he should be someone who wants to work and don't need someone trying to motivate him to do so.

Things like this show character and also the willpower to commit to God and you.

Is he devoted to church?

*P*eople go to church for various reasons: for a breakthrough, for healing, for a partner. You need a man who is devoted to church for the love of God and for the fellowship. He should enjoy going to church with or without you in the picture.

Is he a member of the church (yours or otherwise)?

I have seen men who come to church for the hunt of single females. If he isn't a member of your church or another you should exercise a lot of caution because he may be there to just use women.

Not that men who are members of your church don't do things like that but you may have some historical facts to look at with them. The best predictor of the future is past behavior.

Is he actively involved in the church?

A man who is a champion of God will always want to be a champion for you. There is so much to do when you commit to doing work in the ministry it shows your love for God. I rarely see a man who is committed to God and His Word who is never big on family.

Does he spend time daily in the worshiping of God, and also growing in his faith?

*H*e can always fake it on church day that one day

of the week but you should see him always being a man of faith, not that he should be a fanatic and quote scriptures after every word.

Is he a friend you can count on?

*M*ake sure he isn't someone who always needs

you to be there for him but whenever you need him he is never there.   Don't make any excuses for his behavior it is what is.

When you are committed to him nothing is too hard for you and no matter what you make time for him he should see you with the same amount of importance.

Is he forthcoming with his finances?

- Does he pay his bills and does he pay it on time?
- Does he have a lot of credit card debt?

These are some of the questions you can ask a man early in the relationship in a non-invasive way to have an idea the type of person you are dealing with.

When you've waited for years watching your friends getting married, going to more weddings than a bridal gown then Mr. right turns up.

He seems perfect, he goes to church you are so thankful that it overpowers the uneasy feeling you are getting about the relationship and where it's heading.

Sometimes the feeling you are getting is Gods spirit showing you what you are to avoid.

Here are some of the things if you see him doing or not doing you should start looking again:

If he is a one day Christian

The reason you started to go out with him was that

you loved how he embraced the word.

The way how he loves God, just the type of man you are looking for to make a husband.

He has all the qualities you like but as soon as church is over and he leaves the building he no longer hungers for the word.

No one knows that you are dating him

He tells you that he hasn't told anyone about the

relationship because he doesn't want people in your business.

He doesn't want you to sit with him in church because of what people might say.

You also may hear rumors that he is dating someone else but you would rather think it's false because you think you can't do better because of your age.

Every time he sees you it's about sex

I know you are thinking that at your age it's great

that a man finds you attractive and you may want to sleep with him to stop him from leaving.

But chances are he is doing it with other women in the church.

If he is a man of God he would make sure he marries you first. If your dates seldom end without sex look out.

He has more excuses than you can count why he doesn't want to get married as yet.

Each time it's something different whether he isn't financially ready or he doesn't think you are ready.

Or it's not the right month, whatever it is don't accept his excuses, think about it if you are sixty do you think you can live until you are one hundred and twenty?

Thought so, that simply means you would have more past than future, therefore, you have no time to waste on a dead-end relationship.

Move on if he came along others will, sometimes it's the man you are holding on to that blocks the one that wants to hold you.

Is It Right To Remarry?

I thought I had found my Boaz but………

Is it a sin to remarry?
This is a question that a lot of Christians struggle with especially women.

Sometimes if you stay in an abusive marriage just because you want to stay married you could be living a lie or worst end up dead.

Rhonda was enjoying her marriage, Patrick was the catch of the church he was tall and had an athletic body all the women wanted him.

"Why is it that all these single women won't leave married men alone?"

Rhonda's question was one laced with frustration, disgust, and anger. I knew not to answer because she just wanted to talk.

"I got married when I was twenty-two years old, young and excited about life," she was packing away plates that had just been washed from the weekly feeding program that we volunteered at.

Her husband Patrick was the choir director at the church, he was very quiet and for a fleeting moment, I had wondered what it would have been like married to him.

"We soon started our family, we have four children together. He came home one day and told me that an old girlfriend of his was having some family issues and wanted to stay with us for a while, I agreed; not that I had much of a choice he had asked me with her suitcase in his hand."

She came into our lives like she was a genuine friend. Before I knew what was happening my husband kicked us out divorced me and got married to her. Twenty years and four kids thrown away for some other woman. Now I am at my family's house with four kids and no job.

It is a struggle to survive daily. I am told by other church members that I cannot remarry because it is a sin and if I do I will go to hell.

"What must I do, should I remarry?"

"Is it wrong for me to remarry?"

She was now staring into my eyes and she needed answers.

"Because of the teachings of my church I don't know what to do and there is quite a few church going God fearing men who are showing interest in me."

The questions came fast one behind the other I wished she was in the same mode of rhetorical questions, but now she was waiting for an answer.

Our conversation went on for about another hour I tried to change the topic a few times but wasn't successful. Even when I started to talk about politics she found a way to use a political analogy to compare her broken marriage to it.

The jury is still out on this one but in my opinion if you get married and it doesn't last and you still see the need for companionship. Do you stay single for the next twenty years and wish every day you see your ex turn up in the obituaries?

For me, if it sits well with you, get married again you only live once. Furthermore, if your partner has caused the marriage to be dissolved because of adultery then you are free to remarry

Paradox

We should pursue Jesus Christ and not marriage.

The truth is, if and when the time comes for us to get married, God will allow that love story to blossom into what is right in His sight.

We should focus on serving Him and live our life for Him, thinking about marriage on a constant basis will only cause it to elude us. The timing and correlation are all up to Him and not you or me.
Why am I so sure?
I am truly convinced that we should be fully dependent on God in every area of our lives, including where our relationship/marriage is concerned.

Jesus left us an example to follow
1 Peter 2:21 (NIV)

To this you were called, because Christ suffered for you, leaving you an example that you should follow in his steps.

Jesus never did anything that was of His own, the only thing He did was what was instructed to Him by His Father.

In John 5:19 Then Jesus answered and said to them, 'Most assuredly, I say to you, the Son can do nothing of Himself, but what He sees the Father do; for whatever He does, the Son also does in like manner'".
Jesus at every turn of His life was dependent on His Father for guidance. It wasn't that He couldn't make decisions for Himself but He chooses to be solely dependent on God for everything he did, every word He spoke was of God.
Trusting God to organize our relationships doesn't mean we will have to avoid men or avoid friendships with the opposite sex altogether.

You must spend your life serving

*B*eing single and especially over forty can be overwhelming, but you should spend your time and energy serving God. Even though this may sound controversial, being unmarried gives an amazing opportunity to serve the Lord without any form of distraction.

1 Cor 7:34 lends to such a pronouncement.
God has not called us to build our lives around the pursuit of our own selfish desires but to be poured-out sacrifices for His kingdom.

The big problem that is plaguing us as mature Christian women when we are single is, we get preoccupied with self. We start to seek our own happiness in search of a husband, we get consumed in seeking a companion, which is sometimes not what God has planned for our lives. We all will not find our Boaz but it is much more important to find God so that we can truly find our purpose.

Are there any good single God-fearing men left?

*D*o you think about men and wonder if any good

ones are left? Let's face it being over forty and looking for an age-appropriate mate isn't like the easiest thing. Thoughts that may come to your mind are:

Where are they? And I don't just want a good man, I want one that is God fearing; you may even think that no one is even good enough.

I would tend to agree because we all know how good God is, sometimes trying to find a Christian man to marry can leave you disappointed. A lot of them are not living a Godly Christian life, they don't have the love for Christ that they should have. But what you should take note of is, outside of the church, there are a lot of single men that are unsaved who are pursuing a relationship with God, who would get a better relationship with Him the moment they meet you.

The so-called experts and researchers have attempted on numerous occasions to check how many single women versus single men over forty are in the church and they have always come up on the wrong end.

Reason being they are always relying on man-made tools to check what they are doing but Gods math is much different from ours.

In Judges 7 God used Gideon's army of 300 men to defeat an army of several hundred thousand. Because of this and other numerous facts in the Bible you have to agree that as long as you are on Gods side the advantage is in your favor.

When you look around and you don't see a lot of single men over forty at your church don't stress about it, he might be in another church and God is getting him prepared for you.

Spend your time serving God and stop searching. If you are a single Christian woman today, and you haven't reaped much success in finding your Boaz, take a step back. God has a much stronger call on your life than to have you using all your time and energy on finding the right Christian man.

What is the best way to find a Godly marriage partner? The best way is to stop hunting one. If God wants you to be married He is more than capable of bringing Boaz in your life in the most unlikely ways and also in the most unlikely places.

I have seen Christians who had their love stories written in the most unlikely places.

Am I Too Old?

You may think your time has passed and you have gotten too old for love or maybe you think you are too old to attract a man.

Do you think you are too old to find love?

Think again!

It was George Burns who said we can't help growing old but we can stop being old.

If you are over the age of 40,50 or over 60 you may think you are too old to find love but think again.

The unfortunate truth is many people think this is so and single Christians are at the top of this list. They think that they are too old to find a Godly mate.

"I am too old to find love" that is a lie a lot of Christians speak into their lives and it should be denounced. My faith wavered many times when I thought about my life, I thought this lie was true.

This lie I should not have believed because of other older Christians that I know.

Mr. Francis who is now deceased had women sending him messages when he was in his 80s. He lived a fulfilling life and never passed up an opportunity to dance.

Mrs. James a church sister who always looked as if she just won something lost her husband when she was in her late 70s and she had suitors within months of his funeral.

It was rumored that two of the pallbearers were among the men who were seriously interested in her. Another church sister got married for the first time when she was 68.

You are as old as you feel. Give love a chance don't shun every man that approaches you and then go home to your lonely house asking God to send someone to you when you are sending them away.

What if your Boaz has died?

*W*hat do you do if your Boaz has died? Should you forget about love? You are still very attractive, men are always looking at you salivating like the wolf who ate grandma. You may think that this it, but as long as you are breathing it means life isn't finished with you yet.

Linda's story

It was last June, there was an attractive, almost naked computer analyst in my bathroom, I really wanted him to leave. I'd met him at an Information

Technology Function, he had suggested we meet some other time in a not so business-like setting. We met a couple evenings and had drinks. On this particular night, we had agreed that we would "do it," but as soon as I got to my house I wasn't feeling excited and sexy anymore all I felt was discomfort I wanted him to leave.

I told myself that this wasn't what I wanted, but seriously what did I expect? I was trying to live alone for the first time in my life at the tender age of 63.

I lived with my mom until I graduated from university at the age of 26. I left mommy's house and moved in with my boyfriend George who later became my husband. I lived with George until he died of pancreatic cancer.

After his death, I was left confused and out of sorts. What should I do with myself I always cooked for George now who do I cook for?

 I can't prepare meals for me and me alone?

What happens to your life when you have lost your soul mate? You will think about the good times and the bad times, but it is extremely difficult to deal with the harsh reality that confronts you. Life will throw you some unexpected curve balls but you must try and prepare yourself in the event something like this happens to you.

I loved life I wanted to do so many things but why bother? I hated living alone. It was even worse at nights. I missed having someone to cook for, who would ask me how my day was? Going to bed was even worse, each night, I could feel how cold and empty it had gotten I had to start dating…..at least that is what I thought could fill the gap.

I dated a few guys, but it may have been the fact that I was comparing them to George that they all fizzed before they even got started. Most evenings I was home texting men I either met on the road or at some function, this was done to avoid feeling isolated and alone in my now empty house.

The feeling of emptiness never got better, as much as I loathed living alone. The excessive dating was not helping. How could I force myself into someone else's life that seemed perfect for me?

Why should I try to fit a man into mine? All that effort just to avoid sleeping alone at nights.

How could I fight all these feelings?

I decided to focus on more volunteering and making new friends so I wouldn't be alone as much. I started reaching out to people. My plans were made so that even if I may be lonely now I'll have friends around in the next few days.

I joined my church's community outreach program I started to help feed the homeless. I discovered a joy and fulfillment in doing this, the more less fortunate people I came around the more I realized how blessed I was. I started appreciating coming home alone to my house.

Although I am slowly starting to feel a sense of purpose inside, my house still represents loss. I sometimes feel sadness overpowering me when something great happens and I can't share it with him.

Trying to just pick up any man to fill this void cannot work. My husband dealt with all of the home repairs. Now he is gone I have to figure this out all by myself.

I used to call friends as soon as something goes off track but I am now figuring out these things on my own.

I now look at living alone as me learning some valuable life lessons. At this point in my life, God wants me to be alone, this will make me more independent of men and more dependent on God. I now panic less, I just pray and meditate more on the word of God as he strengthens me daily.

Discovery

After prayer and deep introspection, I have figured out that finding a man isn't the solution to my loneliness. Even though I am dating someone presently I will not settle for him because I am lonely or I need to feel complete.

I have now changed my attitude I have learned to deal with being alone. I remind myself every day of how lucky I am I have a lovely house and I am financially secure. I have been blessed with 37 wonderful years with a man I truly loved who also loved me unconditionally. I feel very lucky and blessed to start a new chapter in my still very promising life.

Is he your potential Boaz?

When you meet allow him to do most of the talking that will make you know him better plus when you ask a lot of questions he will just tell you what you want to hear.

$\mathcal{I}$f you want to get to know him don't ask him any questions that way he can't lie to you or be deceptive.

How can you fight an enemy you cannot see or identify; if you don't tell him what you are looking for then he can't create himself just to sleep with you.

$\mathcal{A}$llow him to be himself you can then decide if he is worth your time. Listen to every word he is saying and what he isn't willing to say.

ever discount yourself you know what you are

worth.
A man will discount you if you allow it. Never settle for less, because you know your value.

ever have sex with him because you want to

please him or to prevent him from leaving that never works. If you saw an apple on a tree and you really wanted it if you shook the tree and got it would you still stay under the tree?

$\mathcal{B}$e yourself no matter what let him know who you are from day one regardless of how tempting it gets. NEVER EVER be someone you are not.   If he doesn't like you well, guess what?
You won't like him either.

$\mathcal{D}$on't play mind games with him if you like him let him know a good man will stay around because he knows you are interested.

Don't play as if you are not interested for him to pursue you, some men especially the ones that really like you may just accept your no because of how much he likes you.

The deceptive ones always love the thrill of the chase because often times they have quite a few women they are "working" on so it doesn't matter how long it takes they don't care.

Don't think it makes you look cheap or desperate to let a man know you are interested, what's the worst that can happen; he tells you he doesn't like you the same way?

$\mathcal{B}$e careful when you start going out with him only give what you get you can't convince him to fall in love with you.

The key is Reciprocity never lose sight of the person that really matters. You.

*A*lways take care of yourself first and love yourself no matter what. If a man is willing to live without you then you can live without him too.

The one who loves the most gives up their power in the relationship so make sure you don't love too fast.

*I*f he can do without calling you all day well, make sure you do without hearing from him too.

If he can't see the value in you then why would you want to be bogged down with a man like him?

*M*ake yourself easy and fun to talk to, be the person he is willing to tell everything. Stop complaining leave your past where it belongs. Think about this, if someone came to you every day and told you about their ex and their sorry and twisted past would you enjoy listening to them? Well, that's the same way someone else feels when you are telling them about yours.

*I*t's easier to obtain than to maintain. When you start dating him NEVER settle, what do I mean? Don't accept him seeing you on some odd days and hours.

If he isn't with you and he can never answer your calls but can call you back sometime later, then don't accept it.
A lot of times it's because he is with someone else so what he does is find a quiet spot to give you a quickie call back.

*D*emand (*not in a demanding tone*) the weekend nights and especially his birthday. If he can't see you on his birthday it's because he is with someone "important".

If he says he is with his mom even better that's where you want to be. You want to meet mom too plus why would he want to spend his birthday with mom she was there when he was born.

*B*e his filling station make sure you are always

listening to his conversations people love to talk and boast about themselves. Encourage it he will love you for it
Make him a king when he comes to you and he will always come running.

*D*on't put him down or embarrass him in front of

others if you have something to say to him wait until you leave that public area. If you always belittle him he will go to another woman who makes him feel like a real man.

*C*ompliment him (*not every waking moment*) but tell

him what you like about him physically and mentally he will always appreciate it.

*N*ever prolong a fight if there is something that is bothering you talk about it and move on. Don't keep bickering about it and don't stay angry it makes no sense because he will prefer staying away to avoid the tense atmosphere. You want your home and the thought of you to be too much to stay away from.

*I*f it's something that he habitually does and it really upset you, keep talking to him about it remember habits don't change overnight.

*D*on't be the first to make up all the time especially if he is wrong because sometimes men will take you for granted. Ignore him sometimes, if he really loves you he will eventually come to you begging for forgiveness.

*D*on't be too eager to please him, if you are the

one who is always trying to please him and he does nothing. Stop and make him work for your affection.

*A*lways communicate with your partner because if

there is none or little in the relationship you will grow apart. If something is bothering you let him know, he cannot read your mind. Sometimes your future

Boaz may be regarded as being selfish because you "thought" he knew you didn't like a certain thing.

Conclusion

As single Christian women, we all have to understand that being single is not a curse and should not be something we try to "GET RID" of.
Sometimes going on a quest to get hitched can lead to more heartache.

Trusting in God to guide us will always put us on the right track.

Chasing a single Christian man most times will not end well especially when you consider anything you chase will always run from you.

I have found myself sitting in church envying married women and sometimes not remembering that not all marriages are happy marriages. Also, there are a lot of married "single" people in the church.

Make the effort to exercise caution when you meet a man because they also know that a lot of us in the church are yearning for a mate.

Take special notice of his body language and the things he finds interest and importance in.

Listen mostly to what he doesn't say because it is more important than what he is saying. Don't lie to yourself thinking he may change, because he is what he is.

The end

Mark 10:6-9

6 "But at the beginning of creation God 'made them male and female.'

7 'For this reason a man will leave his father and mother and be united to his wife,

8 and the two will become one flesh. 'So they are no longer two, but one flesh.

9 Therefore what God has joined together, let no one separate."

THANKS FOR YOUR PURCHASE PLEASE LEAVE A REVIEW ON
AMAZON

Printed in Great Britain
by Amazon